D0343109

HOW TO BE THE
Perfect
GRANDPA

Bryna Nelson Paston

Copyright © 2014 by Bryna Nelson Paston
Cover and internal design © 2014 by Sourcebooks, Inc.
Cover image © RetroClipArt/Shutterstock

Sourcebooks and the colophon are registered trademarks of Sourcebooks, Inc.

All rights reserved. No part of this book may be reproduced in any form or by any electronic or mechanical means including information storage and retrieval systems—except in the case of brief quotations embodied in critical articles or reviews—without permission in writing from its publisher, Sourcebooks, Inc.

All brand names and product names used in this book are trademarks, registered trademarks, or trade names of their respective holders. Sourcebooks, Inc., is not associated with any product or vendor in this book.

Published by Sourcebooks, Inc.
P.O. Box 4410, Naperville, Illinois 60567-4410
(630) 961-3900
Fax: (630) 961-2168
www.sourcebooks.com

Library of Congress Cataloging-in-Publication Data

Paston, Bryna Nelson, 1938-
  How to be the perfect grandpa : listen to grandma / Bryna Nelson Paston.
    pages cm
  (trade paper : alk. paper) 1. Grandparenting. 2. Grandfathers. 3. Grandparent and child. I. Title.
  HQ759.9.P373 2014
  306.874'5—dc23
                          2013045387

Printed and bound in the United States of America.
VP 10 9 8 7 6 5 4 3

Dedicated to Grandpa Alan: If you didn't exist, I would need to invent you! Thanks for being.

CONTENTS

PREFACE

*W*hen you grandpas out there used to be dads, you worked yourselves into a frenzy for years and years and years. You were inside your frenzies and out in your jungles for so long that you sort of ignored your kids who went merrily along under Mom's guidance and care. You checked in every so often to give the kids a hug, inspect their report cards, remark on their growth, and beam at their achievements.

Now you frenzied dads have turned into light-hearted, fun-filled, eager-beaver grandpas who are semiretired or fully retired or semi-fully retired and want to have relationships with your grandchildren.

Okay, okay, hold your horses. Yes, I know that

some dads work hard but also play hard with their kids. And they participate in the daily kid stuff alongside Mom while still making it in the workaday world. I salute you. We are here to address grandpas of all shapes, so get your ticket punched and join the club.

Let's get down to the business of how to be a perfect grandpa. We grandmas who know and love you are perfectly suited to advise on this topic. We know your strengths and weaknesses. We watch your antics with our grandchildren. We offer criticism and praise, whether it's requested or not. We are passionate observers with big mouths. It's our job.

So read and enjoy. I'll give you the inside story on grandpas who are already perfect and those who are still in training. With a little help from my fellow grandmas, grandpas, family, and friends, I've determined that the following rules are true, with a bit of hubris here and there.

The Rules

Show up for everything...and don't forget the napkins!

One hot summer day in New York, Grandpa Alan took three of our granddaughters for ice cream. Now here's the thing about ice cream: Most people like it, but grandpas obsess over it. Grandpa Alan's favorite flavor is mint chocolate chip, and he would move mountains and anything else in his way to get a cone. Kelsey, Amanda, and Alexis were very young but not too young for ice cream. And Grandpa Alan is never too old for ice cream, so everybody was on the same page.

The three little girls came out of the ice cream shop, chins dripping and ice cream melting in avalanches on their clothes faster than they could slurp it up. No napkins.

The girls' mom (our daughter Dina) and I ran back into the store and took a pile of napkins, raced out to the hot mess, and wiped it all up. You see, grandmas have the napkin gene; grandpas do not.

Whether your grandson is batting .600 or warming the bench, you need to be there. Let's say eight-year-old Augie is the best baseball player in the league, the town, the state, the country, and on the planet. Don't just sit there and smile smugly. Jump up and down, and shout appropriate encouragement. (All right, he doesn't need to be told what he already knows, but make your presence felt.) And take him out for ice cream after the game. In fact, take the whole team.*

However, if your little Benjie is

Don't forget the napkins.

destined for greatness in a field other than left, don't just sit there glumly incognito. When he searches for you in the stands, give him a wave and a thumbs-up. Always tell him his moment in the sun is just behind the next cloud, and pile on the encouragement (even if you detest baseball).

Show up, get involved, and of course take him for après-game ice cream.*

A word about taking pictures: Forget the camera; it's so yesterday. If you don't have a smartphone, run right out into the twenty-first century and buy one. Your grandchildren already own them and will teach you how to use yours.

Don't worry, you're definitely smart enough for a smartphone. Trust me.

The tricky part is trying to show your

---

*Well, you know about the napkins by now.

ten thousand photos of your grandson playing shortstop to total strangers. Your success depends on eye-hand coordination: yours and your viewer's.

This would be the point at which Grandma says to nobody in particular, "I just want prints. Nobody will make me prints. You know...to carry around in my purse. Like in the good old days."

You can print out these smart-photos or go to the smart Walgreens people and ask them to do it for you, but that requires knowing how to take the photos in the first place, which gets us back to Step One with the smartphone.

Will someone, anyone at all, please give me prints of my grandchildren playing ball, going to the prom, graduating from high school, or just sitting around looking adorable and brilliant?

One more word about showing up

before we leave this subject: I do understand that some grandpas are living in a foreign country or are in the witness protection program. In that case, you can't show up for anything. So don't.

> *"What a bargain grandchildren are! I give them my loose change, and they give me a million dollars' worth of pleasure."*
> —Gene Perret, comedy writer

Grandpa, answer the call! Babysitter needed!

The biggest and best "show-up" activity for grandparents is, of course, babysitting.

Take Grandpa Erv, for instance, who sadly was widowed last year. Shortly thereafter, his six-year-old grandson

Aiden said, "Poppy, you and I can be together a lot now, okay?"

You bet it's okay. It's better than okay. This child, who was very attached to his grandma, is trying to make lemonade. Grandpa Erv is adding the sugar and stirring the pot as often as he can. He willingly babysits Aiden and his older sister, Devon, and invited his grandson on a trip to go to New York City with him to tour the aircraft carrier *Intrepid*. It's a mere two-hour drive on the turnpike.

"I won't go on a bus," Aiden stated emphatically. "I go to New York on the Acela train."

Another time, Aiden and Devon's parents were on a business trip to the West Coast and asked Grandpa Erv to join them later with the kids, whom he was babysitting. Grandpa Erv was delighted. Aiden declined.

"I won't go with Poppy," he said. "He goes coach, not first class."

So here's the conclusion you could reach about young Aiden and his desire to spend more time with his Poppy. It's fine at home, but when it comes to travel arrangements, they'd better be top drawer all the way.

Grandpa Erv might suggest that young Aiden is a little spoiled, but I prefer to think he is refining his tastes.

"Good old grandsire... we shall be joyful of thy company."
—William Shakespeare, poet,
playwright

Now consider Grandma Olivia and Grandpa Sidney, who were on a long-distance babysitting assignment. They were on hand for a week for the care and feeding of Henry, age eight, and Marcus, age ten.

They had barely settled into the household routine when Henry approached Grandpa Sidney with a deal: he would make their bed for fifty cents a day.

Grandpa Sidney pondered the proposal and said, "How can I be sure you will be the person actually doing the job? *And* will you promise to make a neat bed ready for inspection? *And* what time will you make the bed and how long will it take? *And* I think we should draw up a contract."

By this time Grandma Olivia, on the sly, had given Henry an advance of $2.50 with one condition: He had to play cards with her every night so she had a chance to win back her money. Of course that didn't work because

Grandma Olivia forgot to take a page out of Grandpa Sidney's playbook. She let Henry and Marcus win even when they lost. Grandpa—never!

So the bed-making negotiations continued. Eventually, Grandpa Sidney signed the contract. He was satisfied that all his requirements would be met.

Henry made the bed for three days (or so he claimed). After that he lost interest. Why bother when he was already $2.50 ahead?

Grandma Olivia made the bed for the rest of the week.

Henry has grown up to be a labor union negotiator.

"I never thought about becoming a politician. But during the military dictatorship, my grandfather was put in prison six times and my father,

twice. If my family and my country didn't have a history, I might be a professor today."

—Georgios A. Papandreou, former
Prime Minister of Greece

Rule 3

When changing diapers, breathe through your mouth.

In a *Redbook* **cover** story about the amazing Ivanka Trump and her family, she said her father, "The Donald," loves being included on outings with her and his two-year-old granddaughter, but so far he hasn't tackled the babysitting job on his own.

Ivanka said that her father is a wonderful grandfather, but he really doesn't want to change diapers. But if put to the test, she said, he could figure it out.

Nobody wants to change diapers, I can assure you. And anyone with any smarts could figure it out. As for Grandpa Donald, who is smarter than your average fifth grader, diaper changing should be a piece of cake.

As long as we're on the subject, let's explore the difference between grandpas and grandmas in dealing with bodily functions. Generally speaking, and there are notable exceptions, dads and grandpas will avoid diaper changes and mopping up sloppy spit-up any way they can. (They are not stupid.)

When our kids and grandkids were little, Grandpa Alan would announce: "I think the baby needs a diaper change!"

I was not married to a diaper-changer; I was married to Howard Cosell.

Now fast-forward to present day when all our grandchildren are way

out of diapers and we have acquired a "grand-cat" named Franklin.

Okay, admit it. You have seen photos of and heard about *grand-dogs*, *grand-parrots*, even *grand-gerbils*. I won't say they take the place of grandchildren, but we pamper our pets as if they could.

Of course, there is no diaper-changing issue with pets, just litter boxes or poop to scoop up. In Franklin's case, the poopy box serves its purpose for urinating but is irrelevant for its other intention. Franklin has developed a fascination with pooping in our bathtub, which we never use. (Don't get nervous, we have a separate stall shower.)

I am now the announcer. I smell it. I see it. I yell: "Poopy alert!" Grandpa Alan cleans it up.

That's our deal. I refuse to clean it up.

I cleaned up a ton of dirty diapers in my day. Now it's his turn.

So you see why Donald Trump is such a success in life. He will not deal in dirty diapers, and he won't clean up anyone's bodily functions. I am sure that includes his cat, his dog, and even his goldfish.

Improvise and create.

Rule 4

Grandpa Sy and Grandma Marge were babysitting for an extended period. Their twin grandsons were about two years old and very attached to their twin stuffed elephants. The boys could not, would not, go to sleep without them, and on this night, the elephants were out on safari. After searching the entire house—twice—Grandma Marge

and Grandpa Sy were exhausted but the babies were not. They were busy crying for their animals.

Their mother claims she would've panicked and run to every toy store in town and out of town to find replacements. Not creative Grandpa Sy. He found two tennis balls and two tube socks, put the former into the latter, and drew smiley faces on them, which put smiley faces on the boys. They now had brand-new stuffed animals, and the problem was solved. Everyone got a good night's sleep.

These little twins suffered from colic for what probably seemed like years. Again, Grandpa Sy came to the rescue. He had learned that white noise was helpful. So Grandpa Sy made a cassette tape (remember, this was the good old days) of himself vacuuming for a half hour.

In the background the twins and everyone else could hear Grandpa Sy checking with Grandma Marge: "Is it loud enough, Marge?" and "What do you think about the sound?"

"I think I hear the sound of my husband vacuuming and I am thoroughly enjoying it," she said.

The colic disappeared long before the twins became Columbia University students. They are both classical musicians. I think that started when they heard the "Vacuum Cleaner Symphony in B-minor," by Seymour Beethoven.

Make it happen.

We were on our way home from a wonderful trip out West with our six grandchildren, ages seven to thirteen.

We were in the Minneapolis airport, traipsing along single file from biggest to smallest with our six kidlets schlepping their bags on wheels. It was a Pied Piper scene that other passengers noticed and enjoyed.

We settled in to get food and wait for our connecting flight to Philadelphia. The food was acquired. Our flight was not. Due to bad weather in Philly that day, all flights were canceled.

My job: Keep the kids happy. Grandpa Alan's job: Race through the airport to catch the airport train back to the ticket counter and get us home. This is one big airport, in case you've never been there, especially when you're on the run.

While the kids dove into their chicken fingers and milk shakes, Grandpa Alan spotted a sign flashing "Boarding for

Baltimore." Fortunately, there were exactly eight seats available, scattered throughout the plane. Unfortunately, the plane was leaving in two minutes. Grandpa Alan pleaded his case at the gate. "I have my wife and six grand-children with me who are very young and very tired. My wife's not very young, but plenty tired, too. We need to get to Philly pronto, but we'll settle for Baltimore." He begged as only a grandpa can: "Please, please, please, hold that plane!"

Hold it they did while Grandpa Alan raced back to us in ten harrowing min-utes. He was a little winded and a lot stressed as we gathered ourselves and lickity-split ran all the way back to the Baltimore gate Pied Piper–style. Luckily, we didn't lose one kid.

"Look at it this way," I hollered to

Grandpa Alan en route to the gate. "You have the whole plane ride to catch your breath."

Once airborne, I checked the cabin to make sure all the kidlets were safe, secure, and calm. A kind young woman swapped seats with me so I could sit next to our youngest, Alexis.

As for Grandpa Alan, he started breathing again above Chicago.

But we weren't out of the weeds woods just yet.

"Uh-oh...their parents will be waiting for us in Philly," announced Grandpa Alan. He is very good with announcements. So when we stopped in Pittsburgh, he called each of our kids and invited them to take a two-hour jaunt to Baltimore to meet us, which they did.

All's well that ended well, thanks to

Grandpa Alan. We arrived at our destination somewhat bedraggled. Our luggage? We had no idea. Nor did we care.

Later the following week, the airline invited us to come to the Philly airport and claim our suitcases. Happily, our daughter-in-law volunteered to go for us, armed with a detailed description of everything we had. She and the rest of the passengers on our Baltimore trip spent hours diving through the piles and piles of luggage. Somehow she managed to find and fetch every piece.

P.S. Our trips with our grandchildren, and happily there were several, did not include their parents. That was by design.

However, we were very grateful to our daughter-in-law for her luggage-retrieval efforts.

"More and more when I single out the person who inspired me most, I go back to my grandfather."

—James Earl Jones, actor

When you don't make it happen, the kids will.

Grandpa Winston invited his granddaughter Winifred and grandson Wilfred on a ten-day trip to Italy alone, sans parents. Grandpa Winston was divorced, so no grandma (or girlfriend) was in the picture. The trio had a trying experience.

Winifred and Wilfred were eighteen and twenty, respectively, and thrilled to be going. But all did not go swimmingly.

At meals in the posh hotel, Grandpa Winston persisted in whistling for the waitress every time he needed something. He wanted his Dewar's, and he wanted it that minute.

The kids were mortified. But what could they do? This fabulous vacation was on Grandpa's dime.

When Winifred noticed that the tips Grandpa Winston left were some-what paltry, she took matters into her own hands. As they left the dining room, Wilfred distracted Grandpa and Winifred ran back to the table to increase the gratuity. She did it for breakfast, lunch, and dinner, and by the time they were on their flight home, she was broke and Wilfred had added to the pot as well.

When their parents met them, they asked what Winifred and Wilfred had done and what they'd bought. (We're talking Italy here.)

The kids said they did a lot but

bought nothing. "No souvenirs? Nothing to remember the trip by?" their parents asked.

"Nothing," said Winifred. "We have our memories to remember our truly memorable trip."

"And what about your photos?" asked Mom. "I am sure you took lots of wonderful photos. We can't wait to see them."

"Uh, no," answered Wilfred. "Film is too expensive in Italy, you know."

"But you brought film," said Dad.

"Yes, yes we did, but someone stole our cameras," said Winifred.

"Both of them?" The parents were incredulous.

"Both of them," said the kids with more conviction than they felt.

Later on in private, Winifred and Wilfred regretted that they hadn't taken at least one picture of the tip

that Grandpa Winston hadn't left on
the table.

> *"When I was about three, my grand-*
> *father gave me and my sister a nickel*
> *to sit out on the front porch with him*
> *and sing songs."*
>
>

—*Tommy Shaw, guitarist,*
singer with Styx
>

Make a dream come true.

Our granddaughter Alexis was con-
templating her tenth birthday and
so were we. Grandpa Alan asked
her what she wanted, and she said
without the slightest hesitation, "A
paper shredder."

We were ready for anything—a new
Barbie, a board game, clothes for her

American Girl doll. But no, nothing would do but a paper shredder.

Grandpa Alan stepped up and researched appropriate paper shredders without once asking her what she was going to do with it. Grandma Bryna, on the other hand, said, "What on earth are you going to do with a paper shredder?"

Her parents and sisters were just as curious.

"I am going to shred paper." Alexis announced the obvious to the curious-minded throng.

Grandpa Alan indulged our quirky girl and bought the paper shredder, which was a whole lot less expensive than an American Girl doll sock.

Alexis was ecstatic. Not so much her two older sisters, who had to clutch their schoolwork to their budding bosoms and hide any paper-shredding fuel under their beds. Alexis shredded everything in sight for the next six months.

Grandpa Alan saved all his unnecessary and no longer important paperwork just for her. She was in shredding heaven.

> "A *grandfather pretends he doesn't know who you are on Halloween.*"
> —*Erma Bombeck, humorist*

Zip it up (and I mean your lip)!

There you are, watching a game, recital, theatrical performance, art show, debate competition, tiddle-dywinks match, or any activity that ten-year-old Jerimiah is a part of—and suddenly something annoys you. It's usually that referee or umpire with bad eyesight.

Just because you're old, Grandpa, doesn't give you license to express your opinion. Well, actually it does, but not when a grandchild can hear.

A few years ago during a Little League game, the umpire called Jerimiah out at the plate, even though he slid home with precise timing. His Grandpa Archie saw it very clearly and began yelling at the top of his lungs: "What is the matter with you, ump? That kid was safe by a mile!"

Grandpa Archie jumped out of the stands and confronted the umpire face to face. It was a lot like in the movies: the two gentlemen bumping bellies, poking fingers in the air, and yelling. (I made the last sentence up because I wanted you to get the picture.)

The ump stood his ground. Grandpa Archie was livid, Grandson Jerry was mortified, and it didn't end well. Grandpa Archie was asked to leave the ballpark.

Later than night, Jerimiah asked Grandpa to stay home for the rest of the season. Actually, Jerry asked his coach to trade him to a team in Japan. Then he called Rosetta Stone.

> *"My dad taught me to switch-hit. He and my grandfather, who was left-handed, pitched to me every day after school in our backyard. I batted lefty against my dad and righty against my granddad."*
> —*Mickey Mantle, baseball player*

Grandpa Loose Lips (whom you will meet again in Rule 15) is Grandpa Bradley. He earned his nickname on

many occasions, but especially when he showed up for his grandchildren's sporting events.

To his credit, and we do admire this, Grandpa Bradley was a devoted fan at every game, cheering mightily in the stands.

His daughter Norma says, "He often compared his amazing grandkids to the other players in a rather unflattering way, and he had no regard for the other parents and grandparents sitting near him and clearly within hearing distance. We tried to shush him up but to no avail. What's really amazing is that nobody punched him out."

> *"Every generation revolts against the fathers and makes friends with its grandfathers."*
>
> —Lewis Mumford,
> historian, philosopher

Enjoy your grandchildren, but without decree.

Rule 9

We all recognize that grandpas know better than anybody how to raise children and how to run a small country, but sometimes you just need to stay calm and bite your tongue. Your adult children, married with families of their own, may have noticed that you are the same strict disciplinarian that you always were and that their kids (your beloved grandchildren) don't want the pleasure of your company.

Anita's father, Grandpa Fred, has a summer home in New Hampshire, but her kids don't want to go there even though it's on a beautiful lake that could rival Walden Pond.

"They say it isn't fun. He is so strict and he has so many rules for them,"

Anita said. "I really get it because he was very strict with us—me and my six siblings."

When Grandpa Fred announces he is coming up north from his Florida winter home, Anita's kids know he's about to stop over and they groan, "Oh no, we won't be able to watch TV [in their own home] or go out or anything!"

It's "Make your bed" and "Chew your food fifty times before swallowing" and "Don't interrupt" and "Children should be seen and not heard."

Does he ever do anything with the kids?

"No, I don't think he can relate," said Anita. "When we were little, he took us fishing, but that was because he wanted to go. We picked blueberries with him, but he needed the man-power. He never just sat down and talked to us or told us a story or took us to a ball game or anything."

What's the takeaway from this? Relax, Grandpa. You've got a lot to offer these kids and not much time to offer it. Try to leave the discipline to their parents and learn to enjoy the kids.

As my father used to say, "You'll get more bees with honey, provided you want bees in the first place."

"I don't know who my grandfather was; I'm much more concerned to know what his grandson will be."
—Abraham Lincoln, former president

Recently Grandpa Alan and I were going downtown for dinner and a show with two of our grandkids. We emerged from the train, and Grandpa Alan decided that this was the moment to

point out the old train shed, no longer in use, but an impressive structure that now houses a gigantic convention center in Philadelphia.

One little problem: The guard on duty wouldn't let us walk into the shed, not even a few feet. He diverted us to the written history that was displayed right behind us. This was not good enough for Grandpa Alan, knowing the kids probably wouldn't want to stand there and read. He insisted that the guard let us in.

I would like to point out that this historic building was fairly easy to see from the entrance. It is overwhelmingly large and, like I said, impressive.

The kids and I had really seen enough. We were ready to leave, go outside, and head to our dinner reservation. Not Grandpa Alan.

"Look, they can see very well from here, but I want them to see it better," Grandpa Alan said to the guard. "Just let us in a little farther. A few feet, that's all. You can watch every move we make. This shed has important historic value."

"Sorry, no one is allowed past this point," said the guard. "I must follow the rules."

"What is your name?" asked Grandpa Alan with an edge to his voice.

"Sam," said the guard.

"And what is your supervisor's name?" asked Grandpa Alan with a bigger edge.

"George," said the guard.

"Well, Sam, you just call George right now," Grandpa Alan demanded.

Sam did, and George came. By this time the kids and I were on the escalator to the street.

Sam, George, and Grandpa Alan were sorting it out for God knows how long. The first two wouldn't give in, and Grandpa Alan wouldn't budge.

"It was the principle of the thing," Grandpa Alan said to me later. "I wanted the kids to appreciate what we were looking at."

Meanwhile, I decided that the kids would appreciate a good meal, so the three of us went off to the restaurant and Grandpa Alan showed up by dessert.

Only kidding... He made it just in time to pay the bill.

> *"When I was little, my grandfather made me stand in a closet for five minutes without moving. He said it was elevator practice."*
>
> —*Steven Wright, comedian*

Stay positive, even if it kills you.

My friend's father, Grandpa Martin, traveled more than seven hundred miles to visit his son and family for a few days. When he arrived, he encountered his grandson Virgil, who was sixteen at the time, leaving the house wearing his usual Mohawk hairdo in fashionable orange, with a piercing in every visible orifice. The chains around his low-slung jeans clanked as he walked off the porch.

Grandpa Martin was visibly shaken at this sight. He said, "Where on earth do you think you're going, young man, looking like that?"

Virgil grunted a reply and kept walking, head down. Grandpa Martin tried again. "You look ridiculous, Virgil."

"Hi, Grandpa. Bye, Grandpa," Virgil replied, and he was off.

Grandpa Martin would've done a whole lot better if he'd simply pretended he was at the wrong house.

> *"My grandfather was a voodoo priest. A lot of my life dealt with spirituality. I can close my eyes and remember where I come from."*
>
> —Wyclef Jean, rapper, politician

We have a close friend, Grandpa Mort, (sometimes disguised as TV's Barney— see rule #16 for the rest of the story) who was vacationing in Florida with his wife, Grandma Faith, and three young granddaughters.

One day they went to the zoo. Don't ask me why, but Grandpa Mort was wearing a beige leisure suit, a style that was very fashionable in the '60s. As the family watched, the workers fed the monkeys.

"That's when the trouble started," said Grandma Faith.

After they ate, the monkeys started flying around madly from tree to tree and unloading their dinner on Grandpa Mort and his leisure suit.

"It was all over him—his shoulders, arms, pants," Faith reported. "But nothing fell on me and the girls."

Everyone was laughing hysterically. Well, not exactly everyone.

Grandpa Mort calmly removed his jacket, threw it in the nearest trash can, and said, "It's really too hot for a jacket anyway. Let's go see the elephants. Maybe they'll splash some water on me."

"Grandfathers are just antique little boys."

—Author unknown

Janet's Grandpa Raymond took Grandma Ruth to church on their fiftieth anniversary without saying a word about this special occasion. Afterward he dropped her off and took Janet out to breakfast.

"He didn't forget," said Janet, who is now in her twenties. "He just decided not to do anything about it."

No matter what day it was, Grandpa Raymond preferred Janet's company to anyone else's. To this day Grandma Ruth still brings it up.

Janet's other grandpa, Buddy, expresses his positive approach to life by turning on the TV and turning off his hearing aids. He watches sports for hours without hearing the announcers or Grandma in the background.

"He just nods every now and then, so she'll think he's listening," said Janet.

"But when I come over, he always turns his hearing aids back on."

Obviously what Janet has to say is important to hear.

> *"My grandpa was a wonderful role model. Through him I got to know the gentle side of men."*
>
> *—Sarah Long, actress*

But when it comes to positivity, we must talk about Grandpa Alfred, who was the willing pupil when his five-year-old granddaughter Patty took ballet class. She would come home after each session and teach Grandpa Alfred the steps she'd learned. Then he would actually do them with her.

Patty and Grandpa Baryshnikov pirouetted for hours.

Grandpa Alfred became quite an

accomplished ballerina, but when the New York City Ballet called them to audition, Grandpa Alfred had other plans, like learning how to knit, and Patty was busy being a teenager.

During those years when Grandpa Alfred drove Patty to ballet or softball practice or to a friend's house, he would let her listen to all of her teenybopper music in the car. He never complained about her choice of music, which is something her parents always did.

As the humorist Erma Bombeck once said, "The reason grandparents and grandchildren get along so well is that they share a common enemy."

Do not volunteer for anything that promises to unnerve you.

Sometimes, as the grandpa, you think

you can rewrite history. For example, as a well-meaning and responsible dad, you took your daughter Lucy out to practice driving, and the hair-raising experience left you with a dented fender and a crying need for Xanax. Don't go there with your granddaughter or with your car.

It'll be worse because you are much older now and your patience has worn thin. You really aren't the quick-witted driver you used to be, and according to Grandma, you get lost backing out of the driveway. (I told you about the hyperbole, right?)

The best plan is to leave the driving to your darling granddaughter's parents. Stay home, wave good-bye and good luck from the front porch, and have a martini ready for your son-in-law when he returns...if he returns.

"I spent time in my grandfather Dino's store where he brought in chefs from Naples to cook. I thought they were rock stars."
—Giada De Laurentiis, celebrity chef

Grandpa Alan invited our grandson to a baseball game, and our grandson invited his friend Bert to come along. Bert's mother provided a warning: "Bert usually gets carsick," she said.

Undaunted, Grandpa and the boys piled in his car and off they went. Sure enough, about twenty minutes into the hour-long ride, Bert tossed his cookies all over the backseat.*

Grandpa Alan was prepared with all sorts of cleaners and deodorizers. It took about twenty minutes to get back on the road.

Napkin alert!

At the ballpark, Grandpa Alan refused to buy poor little Bert anything to eat. He was not about to have a repeat performance on the return trip.

The next time and every time thereafter, Bert's father drove to the ballgame.

> *"I had the lunchbox that cleared the cafeteria. Because I hung out with my grandfather, I had sardine sandwiches and calamari that I would eat off my fingers like rings. I also reeked of garlic."*
> —Rachael Ray, celebrity chef

Don't take your grandson fishing if he hates to fish.

Somewhere it must be written that grandpas and grandsons—even

enlightened granddaughters—bond over fishing. You've probably seen that Norman Rockwell painting of a gorgeous summer day with bright sunshine and a perfect blue sky. A very cute grandpa and grandson are standing side by side on the riverbank, fishing poles poised, staring into the water while they wait for something to happen.

And they wait and they wait and they wait. After about six hours of nothingness, the grandson begs to go home, but Grandpa came to fish, and by God, they will fish even if it doesn't happen 'til midnight.

Here's the famous grandpa line (and it doesn't have a fish on it—yet): "No, no, we can't go home yet. The fish are about to bite."

Isn't it fascinating that you rarely see a grandma and a granddaughter standing like statues and not making a sound or moving for six hours? Women simply can't shut up for that long.

I can guess, never having this precious experience and never wanting to, that there is a payoff other than fish. Would Norman Rockwell have wasted all that time and blue paint for nothing?

The thing is, I haven't quite figured out how any bonding goes on if you can't talk or move because you'll scare the fish.

I know I am being terribly unfair to fishing grandpas, and I apologize. You see, we grandmas would rather bond over baking a pie. So would a lot of grandpas. There are even a few dessert cookbooks on the market written by grandpas. (My question is: Did they really write them, or is there a grandma lurking between the strawberry shortcake and the coconut cream pie?)

But I digress.

If you want fish, you can hang around ye olde fishing hole all day and all night with your grandson and talk in the car coming home. Just remember I am not cleaning that fish. Maybe Norman Rockwell will.

Heather's Grandpa Edgar took her crabbing when she was seven. Boys get to go fishing, but girls get to go crabbing—draw your own conclusions.

Anyway, Grandpa Edgar brought his brand-new, very expensive fishing rod to use for the very first time. "He was so proud of it," remembered Heather.

He carefully set it up and was ready to go. You know, going nowhere but ready for the long wait. Just then Heather called him over to see the starfish she had found.

"Grandpa, come here. Come here. I found a starfish. It's beautiful," she shouted.

He ran over to share her excitement, while an enterprising fish on his hook carried his new rod out to sea.

I bet it washed up on shore in Cambodia, and some grandpa there is enjoying his fishing experience with his grandson or granddaughter more than he dreamed possible. Of course it doesn't matter where in the world they are, they'll still have to wait and wait and wait…

There is definitely something going on with this fishing thing. Gloria's Grandpa David loved to fish. He took little Gloria fishing, and she remembers: "We were standing there hoping for a fish or two but, of course, it takes forever. All of a sudden there was this gigantic wave and it knocked Grandpa down. His false teeth washed out to sea."

We can only hope that our Cambodian fisherman on the other side of the world could use a new set of chompers to go with his new fishing rod.

> *"My grandfather always said that living is like licking honey off a tree."*
> —Louis Adamic, author, translator

Share your passion and be passionate about it.

When our grandson Jake was five (and for the next seven or eight years), he was fascinated with tools, fixing things, and locks. Yes, locks of all sizes and shapes. We brought him a gigantic one we found in Hungary at a flea market and he was ecstatic. There must be something going on with our grandchildren: They love paper shredders and locks but have never gone fishing.

Jake's Grandpa Richard is also fixated on fixing. Grandpa Richard lives five hours away, but when he comes for a visit, he comes armed with a toolbox to die for. Jake used to follow him around the house for an entire weekend, hammering and tightening, patching and painting into the wee hours. They even once laid a wood floor. Jake wore his mini tool-belt and looked very professional.

This was serious business. The jobs got done, Mom was thrilled, and Jake was the perfect assistant. Now, years later, Jake is in college rooming with three other guys in a rental apartment. There is plenty to fix, but what's the point? When he isn't studying or playing a sport or seeing the girls across the

hall, his at-home activity extends to clicking the remote and heating up the pizza. Still, all that handyman practice when he was young will look good on his potential husband résumé someday.

Grandpa Alan, on the other hand, collected stamps from a young age, and he tried to tempt our six grandchildren with his passion. He even bought our granddaughter Kelsey a beginner's stamp-collector kit, thinking she would carry on with his hobby. Kelsey has a passion for countries and world affairs.

Good idea, Grandpa Alan, but stamps are too small for Kelsey. She likes the big picture.

I agree. In the early days of our marriage, I used to schlepp to stamp shows with Grandpa Alan because I wanted to impress him. These were held in vast convention centers filled with passionate people tinkering with teensy, weensy stamps.

I'm with you, Kelsey.

> *"You have to do your own growing, no matter how tall your grandfather was."*
> *—Abraham Lincoln, former president*

My friend Gina told me about her father, Grandpa Norman, who was a metal sculptor after-hours. He was sculpting a beautiful candelabrum with his grandson Josh and teaching his craft when Josh burned his knuckles.

Undaunted by singed knuckles, Grandpa Norman took Josh to a captain's boating class. Here was another of Grandpa Norman's passions.

When Josh captained Grandpa

Norman's boat on his own, he lit the oven and it blew up.

"His whole leg was burned because of the back draft," remembered Gina. "But he recovered. So did I. Eventually."

Now Josh is a father himself. The possibilities are endless. But whatever Josh undertakes with his son—and one day, grandson—I would definitely caution against camping trips that require building a fire. Maybe he could teach him how to play poker.

> *"My ancestors started a very dangerous gunpowder business in 1802, and my great-grandfather and his father were both killed in gunpowder explosions."*
>
> *—Pete DuPont, former governor of Delaware*

Join any and all nonsexist, nonpartisan parties.

Speaking of tea, Grandpa, you have to squeeze into that itty-bitty chair in your granddaughter's bedroom and pour imaginary tea into itty-bitty cups while exclaiming, "What delicious tea we're having today. Do you have any cookies to go with this delicious tea?"

Of course she does. You just can't see them, much less eat them. They are usually double chocolate chip.

While you fervently wish that Grandma would quit her touch football game in the backyard with your grandson and come inside to rescue you from this never-ending tea party, it doesn't look promising.

I can remember quite well the gallons of pretend tea we consumed because

we have four granddaughters who were hosting high tea daily. Grandpa Alan was always invited. I am proud to say his manners were impeccable.

> *"My grandfather was remarkably curious about the world, and he read lots of books. He was an important influence in my life."*
> *—Umberto Eco, novelist, philosopher*

Grandpa David, of the drowned teeth, did his best work on land. He owned a thriving flower shop. All sorts of flowers and other plants flourished in the front of the store while waiting for adoption. But in the back of the store, Grandpa David had another gig going. The police on the beat liked to drop in for a card game now and again.

His granddaughter Gloria remembers

the action behind the scenes: "It was a lot of fun for me to go back there and watch," Gloria said. "It seemed like Grandpa and his police buddies were always having a party."

When Gloria matured a little (to about age eight), Grandpa David and the gang invited her to sit in. Of course she needed a couple of lessons, which the detectives provided. Over the years she became quite a polished poker player. Grandpa David was proud. The police squad was chagrined.

Wait a minute…maybe we can get Grandma Olivia and her grandson Henry to come over with Josh and his young son to play poker, and Gloria can teach them the finer points of the game that she learned from the police. Or maybe they would all rather play Monopoly. (See Rule 19.)

"The simplest toy, one which even the youngest child can operate, is called a grandparent."

—Sam Levenson, comedian

Every excursion with Grandpa Ed was a party, at least according to his grandson Greg. Grandpa Ed thoroughly enjoyed life and, more than life itself, the company of his first and only grandson. Grandpa Ed, who lived to be ninety years old, was a jokester who had a story and a punch line for every occasion.

Greg fondly remembers: "Every Saturday morning we had a date at eight. First we had breakfast, and on the way home, we stopped at a store to buy me a toy. As we drove past a golf course, Grandpa Ed would point out all the pretend Indians who were hiding on both sides of the road so we could catch them."

"There's one over there," he'd shout to Greg. "There's another one over there!" And on it went until the golf course disappeared in the rearview mirror.

It's a little difficult to drive and catch Indians, so Greg had to handle their pretend captives. He put them in the backseat and told them to behave.

I know this may not be politically correct by today's standards, but back then, cowboys and Indians was the game of choice for many a youngster. It's important to note that sometimes the imaginary cowboys were the ones captured and put in the backseat.

Hopefully it all evened itself out in the cowboy and Indian universe.

Grandpa Ed regaled Greg with stories about an old Indian chief named

"Strawberry Shortcake." Apparently he got sick and died, and his "squaw buried Shortcake."

"Grandpa Ed was my biggest fan," said Greg, who is now fifty years old with a family of his own. "I miss him every day."

When our cousin, Hugh, became engaged to Leanne, she took him to Montreal to meet her grandpa for the first time. At twenty-two years old, Hugh was a little nervous.

They shook hands, and Grandpa Charlie immediately took Hugh into his bedroom and gave him a shot of whiskey. The two of them had a private party for the rest of the afternoon, and Hugh and Grandpa became fast friends.

Many, many years later when Hugh's granddaughter Sharon became engaged, Hugh stepped right up and offered her fiancé an ice breaker of a drink, only this time it was Courvoisier XO Cognac.

As the party continues, there have been decided upgrades.

> *"There were no distinctive lipstick flavors when Grandpa was a young man. He said when you kissed a girl all you could taste was girl."*
> —**Democrat** *newspaper*
> *(California and Montana)*

Don't always be so darn helpful.

Rule 15

My fellow Grandma Joan and Grandpa Peter have two daughters, Eve and Diana, who are middle-aged now with families of their own. But when Eve was about six years old, she broke her leg.

"She had a cast and crutches, and she was managing beautifully," said Joan. "In fact, we all were. But my father-in-law, Sylvan, kept insisting that Eve needed a wheelchair. We insisted that she didn't.

"But Sylvan insisted louder and one day showed up at our door with a wheelchair," Joan said.

Eve immediately fell out of it.

Grandpa Sylvan had noted on several earlier occasions that Eve wasn't behaving properly.

"He was playing a board game with Eve when she was four, and she had to leave in the middle to go to the bathroom," Joan said. "He couldn't understand why she wasn't more regimented."

According to Grandpa Sylvan, there is a time for the "necessities" and it's not in the middle of any activity.

He watched her coloring and remarked that she was just scribbling when she should be coloring "in the lines."

If Grandpa Sylvan had been Picasso's grandfather, he would have had a nervous breakdown. Nothing that famous artist drew stayed properly in the lines. Eve, however, grew up to be an architect. She lives in a world now that is defined by lines. Grandpa Sylvan must have been a visionary.

Seventy-two-year-old Grandpa Liu Xianping helped his granddaughter with her women's clothing business by posing in the shop's fashions. He quickly became an Internet sensation.

"Why is that unacceptable?" he asked. "Modeling for the store is helping my granddaughter, and I have nothing

to lose. We were very happy the day of the photo shooting. I'm very old, and all that I care about is to be happy."

Check it out, people, he really looks awesome.

Oh, and here's a plus: The store's business increased fivefold since Grandpa Liu's pictures appeared on its website.

As his daughter Nancy was about to give birth, her father, Grandpa Bradley, invited himself into the delivery room lugging his video camera and other assorted equipment.

"We affectionately call my father Loose Lips," Nancy said. "My young, attractive female obstetrician was about to deliver our son Bryan when my father asked, 'When is the doctor arriving?'"

To keep Grandpa Bradley busy, Grandma assigned him the job of videotaping the birth. He had never done this before, and there was no time for instruction, Nancy recalled, so Grandpa Bradley was on his own. Not a particularly good idea.

"When we later watched his recording, we were mortified to find an X-rated show with my private parts as the star," Nancy said. "I am his daughter, after all."

I have heard of other daddies doing the same thing, but not too many grandpas.

Since Grandpa Philip lost Grandma Louise, he has been living with one of his granddaughters, Elinor. Well, he didn't misplace Grandma. She died, sad to say.

The euphemisms for the inevitable—namely dying—always puzzle me. I

especially like "kicked the bucket!" Now what does *that* mean except that you should try to stay away from buckets of any kind and, if you see one, just quietly move on.

Anyhow, Grandpa Philip is safe and secure under the watchful eyes of Elinor and her husband, Warren. The latter have control of the former's finances—with his consent, of course.

Well, there is a slight problem. (When someone says there is a *slight* problem, there is usually a big one). This one is that Elinor is redecorating.

"They are robbing him blind!" reported granddaughter Babs. "But he doesn't seem to mind. Maybe it's because Elinor took such good care of Grandma in her final illness."

Elinor has replaced every carpet, every hardwood floor and every window treatment, every cabinet, every door-knob, every *everything* in her house and on her patio, her siblings say. She has purchased all new major and minor appliances, and she has a brand-new car.

"She has taken all the funds she needs and wants out of his account," Babs said. "We are a very large family. Grandma Louise and Grandpa Philip had seven kids, so there are twenty-two grandchildren and thirteen great-grandchildren. All of us—including our aunts and uncles, nieces, nephews, and cousins—are very upset."

Most of the far-flung family prob-ably wouldn't even know about Elinor's projects, but she puts them up on the Internet for the world to see.

Certain family members confronted her, and she immediately erased every-body from her Facebook page. And I bet they won't be invited over for dinner anytime soon.

Grandpa Philip is not complaining. He is helping Elinor, who is helping him and helping herself to their inheritance. So the rest of the gang can stop counting his money because when Grandpa Philip kicks the bucket, the bucket will be empty.

> *"Unlike my grandfather or my brother, I've actually been able to make some money at a racetrack."*
> —*John Malkovich, actor*

Find your identity, Grandpa, and embrace it.

The grandparenting scene in Los Angeles is somewhat nontraditional.

It's that California laid-back, do-your-own-thing...thing.

"You can see an eighty-year-old grandma driving a Rolls Royce and a ninety-year-old grandpa wining and dining a forty-year-old girlfriend," reports Grandpa Jules, who is a divorce attorney to the stars.

Grandpa Jules has a front-row seat to the LA lifestyle like no other. He reports that there are so many marriages and divorces and unwed mothers who choose to have children minus the father's participation that any family event becomes a logistical nightmare.

Grandpa Jules has a grandson named Jonathan. Jonathan also has Grandpa Howard and Grandpa Nick. (Please don't ask me to explain this. Suffice it to say that, because of all the changes in status among the parents and

grandparents, about sixty people show up to all of Jonathan's events. Well, maybe not sixty, but still an awful lot of people.)

"Everyone is saving chairs for everyone else," Grandpa Jules said. "There is never enough seating."

After one of Jonathan's events, a kindergarten musicale, he said to Grandpa Jules, "Hi Grandpa Howard."

"And I answer, 'I am not Papa Howard,'" said Jules. "Then he takes a closer look and says to me, 'Hi, Papa Nick.'"

"'No, I am not Papa Nick.'"

At this point, Jules's daughter tells her five-year-old son that this is the "one with the money," and Jonathan says with a knowing grin, "Hi, Papa J!"

It takes a long time and a lot of work to sort it all out. The fascinating part is that everyone (the adults) seems to handle the confusion very well. And the kids? They get it. Like I said, this is LA.

I wonder what will happen when another Papa J turns up. He could be a James or a Joe or a Jasper. Name tags might be useful.

"I want to experience everything. Being a husband, being a father, hopefully someday being a grandfather. I want all those experiences so when I die, I want to be exhausted."
—Bryan Cranston, actor

Some grandchildren are lucky enough to adopt a grandpa who fits into the family perfectly but is no blood relation.

Grandpa Ken began a relationship with Grammy Melanie a few years after each of their spouses had died. The two couples had been friends so it was an easy transition.

But the children and grandchildren in both families had to adjust.

"Grandpa Ken and my Grandpa Jack had worked together as engineers," said grandson Benjamin, now in college majoring in a variety of engineering subjects that nobody understands but him.

He didn't accept this interloper as quickly as his older sisters did.

But in time Grandpa Ken established his own identity and was welcome at all family gatherings. Eventually Benjamin came to embrace his "adopted" grandpa because, as his sister Melissa said, "They could talk 'engineer.'"

"We have a symbiotic relationship, I think," said Benjamin, who is allowed to use big words now that he's in college.

We both got the other part of the family we were missing."

> *"The closest friends I've made through life have been people who also grew up close to a loved and loving grandmother or grandfather."*
> *—Margaret Mead, anthropologist, writer*

You could say that our dear friend Grandpa Mort had an identity crisis when his first grandchild, Jessica, celebrated her first birthday. He rented a Barney costume for sixty dollars and showed up at the party. This was twenty years ago when the giant purple dinosaur came cheap.

Jessie screamed in fright and shut herself up in her bedroom. She wouldn't come out. It was chaos. Several other little guests were also freaked out. Barney left, returned the costume, and returned to the festivities hours later—as himself. Jessie was much calmer and overjoyed to see Grandpa Mort.

The truth didn't come out until Jessie was old enough to know, which was last week. She's a junior in college so it's about time they 'fessed up.

> *"My grandfather, Frank Lloyd Wright, wore a red sash on his wedding night. Now that's glamour."*
> *—Anne Baxter, actor*

Be a hero, Grandpa, and do it *your* way.

Grandpa Gil unfortunately became totally blind at the age of forty, long before his grandchildren were on the scene. He suffers from a rare disease that is very debilitating in many ways. He needs assistance all day, every day.

His wife, Grandma Sandy, is his eyes. She takes him everywhere, even to the movies and ball games where she and his kids provide the play-by-play. Grandpa Gil is not one to sit home and feel sorry for himself, and he loves sports.

He has never seen his grandchildren, but he knows them very well. His oldest grandson, Morey, who is a college freshman, sees his Grandpa Gil as his hero.

Morey is an athlete and excels in many sports. Grandpa Gil attended all of his games from Little League through high school, and with help from the sidelines, he pretty much knew what was going on. When Morey was at the plate, the crack of his bat was music to Grandpa Gil's ears. He cheered louder than anyone there.

Morey, who never thinks of his grandpa as handicapped, is studying sports broadcasting, thanks to his years of sitting next to his Grandpa Gil and offering his commentary on whatever sporting event they were sharing.

There is no doubt that grandson Morey's chosen profession was inspired by Grandpa Gil. But the courage and grit that Grandpa Gil shows by living each day as normally as he can is a far greater inspiration.

Grandpa Gil and Grandma Sandy also have a three-year-old grandson who desperately wants to play soccer with his Grandpa Gil. Grandma Sandy told the little one that Grandpa Gil can't see the ball. However, she devised a way for the two of them to make a connection. Bobby places the ball at Grandpa Gil's feet.

Grandpa Gil can feel it and kick it. Bobby runs all over the house chasing the ball. Of course, no one knows where the ball will land, but Bobby always finds it and brings it back. No broken lamps, so far.

Bobby will grow up with his grandpa talking and listening to him and even playing with him, but never knowing what he looks like. Seems to me that's enough to make a hero in Bobby's eyes.

> *"A grandpa is someone you never outgrow the need for."*
>   —*Author unknown*

A hero of a different sort was Grandpa Max, who lived life with a certain joie de vivre that sometimes got him into trouble with the family and the law. But never with his grandchildren.

His granddaughter Judy recalled, "My

Aunt Freda and Uncle Paul and their son Georgie lived with my grandparents. Georgie was a gorgeous two-year-old with a head full of beautiful curls."

Grandpa Max, often referred to as "Pop," decided one day when he was babysitting that Georgie looked too much like a girl. His generation couldn't tolerate such nonsense. He got the horse clippers from his barn where he housed four or five horses who dutifully pulled his wagons in summer and sleighs in winter.

"Pop gave Georgie his first haircut within an inch of his scalp," Judy said. "All the curls were on the floor of the barn."

"When Aunt Freda came home, she was horrified at the scalping Pop had given her darling little boy. She called everyone in the family screaming, 'Oh Georgie, my Georgie, oh no, oh no,'" said Judy. "My mother, who was her sister, thought Georgie had died. It was a calamity then but funny now."

This was not the first time or the last that Pop's antics almost caused one of his daughters-in-law to disown him. No doubt, his grandchildren would have packed up and left town along with him.

There was a big snowstorm in Wilkes-Barre, Pennsylvania, one winter—and every winter, actually. No global warming in that town.

Pop would come over for dinner at his grandson Larry's house, which he did almost every night.

Pop had a huge black Cadillac. "It was the kind where you pushed a button on the taillight and it popped open to put gas in the tank," Larry recalled. "He loved showing everyone that feature."

Pop told Larry's mother, Fanny, that he was taking the child for a sleigh ride.

Since they lived near the park along the Susquehanna River, Fanny assumed he was taking Larry to the dikes, but he had another plan.

"He tied the sleigh to the back fender of his car, and off we went," Larry said. "No, I wasn't in the front seat or even the backseat. I was in the sleigh, bouncing around as we circled our neighborhood.

"Of course no seat belts or car seats back then, which really wouldn't have protected me in the sleigh anyway, but I was fine. So was Pop until my mother came out and took a look at this scene."

After that, Pop was absent from the dinner table for months.

Pop often picked up his nine grandchildren at school with his horse and sleigh in the winter and horse and wagon in the fall and spring.

The first time Pop picked up Larry

from middle school in his horse and buggy, Larry recalled, "I was mortified that all my friends would laugh.

"But no, they were really jealous."

Pop considered himself quite the man about town. Dressed impeccably, usually in a double-breasted blue suit (to match his bright blue eyes) with a Sulka tie, he donned a top hat to ride with his horse and wagon in the Easter parade every year. On an ordinary Sunday, he was more relaxed and wore jodhpurs for his weekly rides. There was always a grandchild beside him.

"Sadly, none of his grandchildren carried his love of horses into their generation," Judy said. "My cousin Howard perhaps loved the horses the most, but he had severe asthma so he couldn't go near them."

One day Pop had parked his horse

and wagon at a meter in downtown Wilkes-Barre. He came out of a store and found a policeman waiting for him, ready to write a ticket.

"When asked his name, Pop replied with his own brand of dignity, 'Max Goldstein,'" Judy said.

A local semi-pro basketball player by the same name lived in Wilkes-Barre but was no relation. The policeman, obviously a basketball fan, asked Pop if he was that Max Goldstein's father.

"Wily Pop answered yes without batting an eye, and the policeman tore up the ticket," Judy said.

Max's problems with the law didn't end there. He was jailed briefly a few times for bootlegging, another one of his careers. When he paid the fine of about $150, a small fortune in those days, he was a free man.

In the eyes of his grandchildren, who didn't know of his escapades until they were adults, he has an untarnished image. Judy and Larry remember Pop as a different kind of grandfather figure, whom they describe as a "Damon Runyon" character, full of fun, a risk-taker, and nothing like their friends' grandpas who were kind and loving but mostly sedentary. He was anything but a typical grandpa. He was their hero and the hero of every kid on the block because he was so full of love and life.

> *"I am very proud of my grandfather's gold pocket watch. On his deathbed, he sold it to me."*
> —Woody Allen, director, producer, actor

My sister remembers our Grandpa Abe much better than I do. That's the reward for being the oldest and first grandchild. Harriet worshipped him and vice versa. He was in the junk business. Today we dial 1-800-Buy-Junk and a junk hunk (a very fit young man of college age) comes to collect our old stuff for resale.

In Grandpa's day—the 1930s—his gigantic warehouse, which was right next to his house, was three stories high and chocked full of treasures for my sister.

"I loved to go over there," Harriet recalled. "Grandpa would let me search the entire place and take almost anything I wanted.

"In the center of the building was a bailer for magazines and newspapers. It was the height of the building—very impressive to a little girl."

Harriet went to the shop to check out

the comic books that came in. "Grandpa would stop his bailers when I was there so I had enough time to find the comic books I wanted and sit there and read them," she said.

Grandpa Abe and Grandpa Max shared a love of big cars. Our grandpa owned a Nash, but he didn't know how to drive.

"He would draft one of his children, whoever had a license, to drive him around town," Harriet said. "I don't know if the car was really big or it was that I was small, but I loved sitting in the backseat, being chauffeured around."

"My grandfather worked with Thomas Edison on the electric car, and he sold electric cars at the 1900 World's Fair in Paris."
—Al Jardine, guitarist, composer
(The Beach Boys)

Our grandpa heroes come in a dazzling array of sizes, shapes, and styles. One such standout is my dentist Mona's grandpa. He was a doctor and his name was Raojibhai Sardar Patel.

As a little girl, Mona, who lived in America, would go back to India to visit.

"My Grandpa Patel was my hero, my inspiration," Mona said. "I loved his books, especially *Darwin's Theory of Evolution*. My favorite page was where the apes morphed into man."

Mona credits Grandpa Patel with motivating her interest in science. "I am sure that's why I became a dentist," she said.

But Grandpa Patel wasn't just about serious subjects like future professions. According to Mona, he would "fake a walk in the park" with her so they could detour to the ice cream store.

"We loaded up on ice cream and all sorts of treats, and nobody ever knew," she said. "We came home and acted like we'd had a lovely walk. I never told my grandma or anyone else."

It might be worth a trip to India to enjoy those unusual flavors that Mona remembers so well: pistachio saffron, cashew raisin, and falooda (rose).

I am leaving right after this sentence.

"I was taught by my grandfather that anything your mind can conceive, you can have. It's a reality."
—*Lenny Kravitz, singer, actor*

Don't be another grandma.

Jump in here, guys, and prove your worth. Some grandpas, and you know

who you are, simply let Grandma take the lead. Pushy, aren't we?

When we say, "Let's go see the kidlets," you go. Then it's off to whatever activity we're in the mood for or we think the kidlets will enjoy.

No, no, no, and no! These grandkids want to spend solo time with you doing stuff that Grandma wouldn't dream of. For example, have a session on the stock market or tie some knots like you did at Boy Scout camp. How about a skydiving lesson? Or spelunking? This grandma wouldn't consider that in a million years.

You could always teach your grandchild how to make your secret recipe for chicken cordon bleu. I know, I know, but truly enlightened grandpas can pull anything off. And truly enlightened grandmas will let you.

It will be a great lesson in clean-up, too—probably for Grandma.

> *"I grew up, as many Indians do, in an archipelago of tongues. My grandfather was a surgeon in the city of Madras (India). He was fluent in at least four languages and used each of them daily."*
> —*Aravind Adiga, journalist*

When our first grandchild, Rachel, was about to come into this world, I was eagerly awaiting that glorious summons from my son Michael. The phone rang at 6 a.m. and he said, "We're going to the hospital now." So I jumped in the car and sped along, pulse racing, to meet them there. I don't think I drove that day; I flew.

I went alone because Grandpa Alan had to go to work.

"How can you do that?" I screamed.

"Well, if I go to the hospital right now, that won't make the baby come any faster," he answered calmly.

"Of course it will," I snapped. I went. He made his entrance a couple hours after our babycakes did. This explains our different approaches to life. I gallop, he strolls. Rachel was born forty-five minutes before I arrived, and when I hugged the new daddy, it was one of my most beautiful moments ever (plus holding that newly hatched baby was the thrill of my life).

Memo to Queen Elizabeth II: I get that you "don't do hospitals" so you couldn't or wouldn't just hail a cab and get over there the minute that baby prince, your great-grandson, came into this world.

But while you were sitting with your

corgis in that comfy, ginormous palace, I bet anything that *Great*-Grandpa Prince Philip snuck into the hospital via the kitchen, made his way through the corridors and up in a private elevator (sealed off just for him!), and took a little peek.

Sometimes it's not really good to be the queen.

One spring day our grandsons Jake and Matt, ages ten and seven, came over to entice Grandpa Alan into a baseball game. Our backyard was perfectly flat and big with lovely perimeter trees and plenty of space for any athletic activity.

"Oh, I am so happy to see you boys," I said with hugs all around. "But unfortunately Grandpa Alan is busy mowing the lawn right now, so no game for a while."

"When do you think he'll be done?" Jake asked hopefully.

"Not for a long time, sweetie pie," I replied. "You know our lawn is big."

So I suggested we jump in the car and go for ice cream. I sent Matt out back to see if Grandpa wanted any. (What a silly question.) He came back in two minutes with this report: "You should see Grandpa's lawn mower. It's mowing all by itself."

"Oh, I don't think so, Matt," I said, but I looked out the window.

Yikes! Grandpa Alan wasn't mowing the lawn at all. The mower was mowing unattended, going round and round in circles from a center post on the lawn. Grandpa was sitting on the patio reading the newspaper.

I ran outside with the boys trailing right behind me. Sure enough, it was an incredible picture. Grandpa Alan was stretched out on the chaise with the

New York Times open to the business section. The lawn mower was doing an amazing job on its own.

Grandpa Alan's industrial engineering background had come into play. He had attached our power mower to a post in the center of the lawn with a very long rope that was wound around the post. He had started the mower and guided it to unwind the rope, thus mowing in perfect circles all over the entire lawn.

"Alan! How do you know it's not going to break away and travel off?" I asked Mr. Nonchalance.

"I'm watching," he said calmly.

The kids loved it, but just as we were patting Grandpa on the back, the mower rope broke, and the lawn mower took off. Traveling solo, it mowed a big stripe through our neighbor's yard and

his neighbor's yard before the boys could catch it.

Jake and Matt still tell their friends about Grandpa Alan's self-mower. I am telling my friends about how Grandpa's ingenuity allowed him to rest and relax while I was in the house vacuuming with a Grandma pushes-it vacuum. The boys had their game after all. And that freshly mowed grass sure helped anyone sliding into second base.

> *"I was getting worried I may not become a grandfather, but the Lord has blessed me."*
>
> —Rod Stewart, singer

Rule 19   Grandpa's dos and don'ts list.

(Don't worry, Grandma, we'll get to

your list in a minute. After all, this book is about grandpas, you know).

- Do tell them about your childhood.
- Don't discuss your jail time.
- Do read them stories. It's a great way to get a nap—yours.
- Don't read any story that begins: "It was a dark and stormy night…" (They won't get scared; you will.)
- Do call them on birthdays no matter how old you or they get.
- Do sing "Happy Birthday" to them on the phone.
- Don't do it in person unless you are Bob Dylan.
- Do show them how to make a perfect fire and tie a perfect bow tie. (Don't do these things at the same time.)
- Do teach them how to grill a steak

and how to carve a turkey. (Don't do these things at the same time.)

- Do tell them how to bet on a horse.
- Don't take them to the track until their parents are out of town.
- Do take the boys to buy their first suit.
- Don't take their parents along; they know nothing about proper shoulder-fit.
- Do throw your babies up in the air.
- Don't forget to catch them.
- Do chase your grandkids around the house, neighborhood, and town.
- Don't lose anybody.
- Do wrestle anyone over nine years of age but smaller than you.
- Don't overdo. Remember: Your back is old, theirs is young.
- Do play any sport they want anytime, anywhere, at a moment's notice.

- Don't offer to teach them any sport unless you are Charles Barkley.
- Do take them to parades and ball games.
- Don't lose them.
- Do start a Monopoly game with them when they are two and continue it until they go to college.
- Don't ask "Who wants to play a little Monopoly?" There is no such thing as a "little" Monopoly.
- Don't invite Grandma to play because she'll be screaming: "Take my railroads, my utilities, my Boardwalk. I am bored silly and I have to go to the bathroom."
- Do dress up for Halloween. You might get a Snickers bar.

Speaking of dressing up, we had an elegant dinner party once with all six

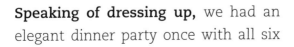

of our grandchildren at the table. The rules were that we all had to dress up, so they raided our closets. Grandpa wore his long, blue kimono from China with a dragon on the back.

The kids graced the table wearing all sorts of wild creations in the guise of such characters as an artist from the Left Bank, a fashion designer, a princess, a multimillionaire poker player, a lion tamer, and more.

The menu was stunning: chicken fingers, miniature hot dogs, and all the pasta you could eat, topped off with self-styled ice cream sundaes that toppled over from the weight of hot fudge, nuts, marshmallows, peanut butter sauce, and bananas. Everything was served on china with crystal stemware for lemonade.

My closet looked like a tornado had just swept through, as did Grandpa's.

Our kitchen was a complete mess.

Grandpa didn't care. He had napkins. Linen. Embroidered.

Leave it to Grandma.

Rule 20

- Shopping.
- Slopping on makeup.
- Doing manicures and pedicures, even for boys.
- Trying out new hairdos.
- Telling stories with a lot of drama.
- Reading stories with a lot of voices.
- Making up silly songs.
- Playing any board game but... Well, you know.
- Making hot fudge sundaes.
- Staying up all night to watch movies on TV while eating sundaes in bed.
- Slopping up the kitchen to invent a new dish.

- Having "pots and pans parades" around the house, neighborhood, town.
- Going on "listening walks."
- Allowing grandkids to dress up in her shoes, clothes, or anything else in her closet, which stays open 24/7.
- Allowing granddaughters to borrow jewelry for the prom.

"My grandfather once told me that there are two kinds of people: those who work and those who take the credit. He said to try and be in the first group. There is less competition."
—Indira Gandhi, third prime minister of India

Rule 21

Some assembly is required.

The fastest way to get rid of Grandma is

to ask her to put something—anything—together. Generally speaking, of course, grandpas just love to spend hours poring over directions. Most grandmas couldn't care less. When your son invites you over for dinner, beware! He needs assistance but actually you'll be the one needing assistance. A good barometer of how many things need to be built, fixed, adapted, realigned, or re-imagined is in direct correlation to who does the inviting and when.

If the invitation is hand delivered by your son or son-in-law after December 25 and before January 15, there is work to be done: furniture to build and toys to assemble.

If, on the other hand, the invitation comes three days or more in advance and it's from your daughter or daughter-in-law, Grandma will say: "We'd love to

dear. What are you having?" And the answer is: "Whatever you're bringing."

The only intelligent thing to do is eat out. So Grandpa is either in charge of construction or in charge of the check.

"My grandfather helped draft the first constitutions of China. He was a fairly well-known scholar."
—Maya Lin, architectural designer

In the early stages of grandfathering, you'll be carrying the car seat, which must be attached to your car's backseat. No car seat, no baby. That car seat is a monster, a cumbersome accessory that was invented by someone who hated grandparents. Just try taking it on a plane. I dare you.

The fun really begins when you try to attach a squirming two-year-old to the car seat, which you have just attached to the car. My advice is to start this field trip seven hours before you really need to. The extra time is invaluable because it gives you at least an hour of cursing, which you can only do if the child in question doesn't understand what you are saying.

And furthermore, you need to carry a stroller, a Pack and Play (which is a down-sized playpen), a collapsible high chair, and, later, a potty seat. You can count on Grandma to bring a bunch of toys and a diaper bag stuffed with a change of clothes, diapers, baby wipes, a bottle, and later in life (the child's, not yours) a sippy cup and Cheerios.

I would now like to discuss this Cheerios phenomenon. What person in charge of cereals decided a hundred

years ago that babies could pick up Cheerios easier than any other brand, and the message came down to all mothers, grandmothers, fathers, grandfathers, aunts, uncles, cousins, nieces, nephews, and assorted babysitters that "Cheerios are especially designed for little fingers."

Because, dare I say, it has nothing to do with taste. Cheerios taste like little, round twigs.

I know. Don't fret. I am up to date on my Cheerios news: They now cheerfully come in tutti-frutti flavors, even chocolate, but they still taste like something that nature forgot.

But every little person has a little lidded container that goes where he or she goes so they never run out of Cheerios.

Everybody knows that at some point in the baby's life, you have to stock up.

But by the time the kid is five, Cheerios are gone.

Can you name anyone over the age of five who eats Cheerios? No, not even Grandpa.

I can hear you out there...yes I can... saying: "My uncle Arthur eats Cheerios."

No, he doesn't. Not as a steady dish that captures his morning. Nope. I won't tolerate fibbing. Maybe Arthur accidentally finished off the leftover Cheerios from two-year-old Lilly's breakfast when nobody was looking, but as a steady diet choice, no way!

Grandpas prefer corn flakes in the summer and oatmeal in the winter. Farina, too.

Now, where was I? Oh yes, loading up the car for that cross-country trek or down the block to visit a friend. If

Grandma has left you on your own, just man up. A U-Haul is required at that point, and the good news is that you, Grandpa, are the You-Haul.

You will be heard to say at least six times: "I can't believe one little baby needs all this stuff." Then you will say at least six times: "Our kids didn't have all this stuff when they were little, did they?"

It does get easier, though, when they are about seventeen. Just give them the car and be grateful you don't have to put it together first.

Grandfather Mountain in North Carolina State Park is 5,946 feet at its highest peak. It's in the Blue Ridge Mountains, one of the major chains of the Appalachian Mountains. Blue Ridge Parkway passes by the south side of

Grandfather Mountain and also over nearby Grandmother Gap.

I rest my case.

> *"If you want to know where I come by the passionate commitment I have to bringing people together, without regard to race, it all started with my grandfather."*
> —Bill Clinton, former president

Grandpas are a wealth of information.

Grandpa knows which came first: the chicken or the egg; why anyone in his right mind needs to find X, and where it's been hiding all these years; and why a pound of feathers weighs more than a pound of peanut butter. (I made that one up!)

Grandpa knows why dark chocolate tastes better than any other kind and why, in a random group of twenty-five or more people, two will share the same birthday. (Trust me, this works!)

Grandpa knows why the ocean never stops, how they built the Holland Tunnel, why we should pay attention to the stock market, why you should always serve food on a warm plate (unless of course the food starts out cold), why you should never buy gas in a station owned by Hugo Chavez, and why everyone in Congress should be voted out of office—and he means everyone!

Grandpa knows how a GPS knows where you are and where you should go and the best or fastest way to get there without yelling at Grandma, who told you to turn left at the last intersection.

Grandpa knows why you turn on a TV and immediately leave the room. (Answer: To drive Grandma crazy.) And why you would turn on every light in the house and go outside.

Grandpa knows the best diet is eating half of everything on his plate. He lets Grandma eat everything on her plate and half of his. Ergo, he's disciplined, she's not.

Grandpa knows that it's only possible to buy a new car after the old one, which was on life support at 97,000 miles, drops dead 97 miles from civilization.

Grandpa knows usually, most always, infuriatingly, the answer to

any question on old train sheds, geography, science, math, sports, current events, puts and calls, groundhogs, or stamps...and claims he doesn't. Just give him three minutes while he thinks. (I am certainly not saying that Grandpa is smarter than Grandma... Well, not when it comes to napkins anyway.)

Grandpa knows why a grandfather clock is not a grandmother clock.

Now you can know, too. The grandfather clock was invented by William Clement in 1670–71. It had a long, tall case and originally it was called...wait for it...a clock. How inventive was that?

Then in the 1900s they were called grandfather clocks because they belonged to a bygone era when they were made with a great attention to decorative aesthetic detail. I hate to argue with history, but "decorative aesthetic detail" seems more feminine than masculine so I am starting a grassroots movement to rename every single one, no matter how tall, a "grandmother clock."

> *"My grandfather gave me my first guitar, an old acoustic with palm trees and dancing girls painted on it."*
> —Dan Fogelberg, singer

Learn the gifts of the seven grandfathers.

Rule 23

The Anishinaabeg Indians teach that the path to healthy living and community survival is in the following collective. You can't have one without the others.

- *Minwaadendamowin*: Respect
- *Zaagidiwin*: Love
- *Debwewin*: Truth
- *Aakodewewin*: Courage
- *Nibwaakaawin*: Wisdom
- *Miigwe'aadiziwin*: Generosity
- *Dibaadendiziwin*: Humility

The tribal elders confirmed that when all seven are a part of you, you are *Minobimaadiz*—living a good life. Don't get any ideas. If you only embrace six out of seven, you will suffer the opposite of the one that's missing. For example, if you are not a wise person, ignorance will consume you.

And all the respect, love, truth, courage, generosity, and humility in the world won't save you. The origin of the gifts of the seven grandfathers is unknown. Suffice it to say that they are beautiful Indian words that express simple but important themes.

Follow these seven easy steps to grandpa perfection.

Rule 24 to forever

- Keep calm.
- Laugh a lot.
- Love a lot.
- Make memories.
- Try to stay out of trouble.
- Don't take yourself too seriously.
- Keep Grandma's number on speed dial.

*B*ryna Nelson Paston is an overjoyed grandmother of six, ages sixteen to twenty-three, and she wonders how they all had the nerve to grow up while she had the nerve to grow old. Her very successful first book, *How to Be the Perfect Grandma,* is still sell-

ing worldwide. Formerly a newspaper editor and writer in Philadelphia, she gave all that up when her grandchildren arrived. She has written for national magazines and newspapers. Bryna (rhymes with china) has also written and published multiple children's plays. She is a part-time actor and avid bridge player. She lives in Elkins Park, Pennsylvania.